Mad About Meyer Lemons

Mad About
Meyer Lemons

Written and illustrated by
A. Cort Sinnes

Hearth & Garden Productions
Napa, California

Printed in the United States of America

Hearth & Garden Productions
P. O. Box 571
Napa, California 94559

This book was designed and produced by
Hearth & Garden Productions
A. Cort Sinnes, Text, Design and Illustrations

Library of Congress Cataloging-in-Publication Data

Sinnes, A. Cort
Mad About Meyer Lemons, written and illustrated by
A. Cort Sinnes

ISBN 978-0-692-59584-8

For Frank N. Meyer,
for all he did to make this a more
beautiful and delicious country

Table of Contents

Above: The Great Wave Off Kanagawa, *Hokusai's most famous work.* Left: *Katsushika Hokusai, self-portrait.*

Above: *One of Rivière's* 36 Views of the Eiffel Tower. Left: *Henri Rivière.*

Artistic Obsession

I think it's safe to say that most artists are obsessed to one degree or another. More rare is the artist obsessed by a single object; Monet and his haystacks comes to mind (in 1890, he painted 25 paintings of them in differing light and atmospheric conditions). But Katsushika Hokusai (1760 - 1849) and Henri Rivière (1864 - 1951) win the prize for being the most obsessed by a single object: In the 1820s in Japan, Hokusai produced what he called *36 Views of Mt. Fuji.* Inspired by Hokusai, some eighty years later in Paris, the artist Henri Rivière painted *36 Views of the Eiffel Tower.* Reproductions of both the Mt. Fuji and the Eiffel Tower woodblock prints paintings proved immensely popular with the art-loving public on a world-wide scale.

I wouldn't say I'm obsessed with 'Meyer' lemons, but I *am* deeply impressed by them. For me, they embody an effortless perfection and the very essence of the joy of living in a cli-mate like that of California. The heavenly perfume of their delicate flowers, the distinctive aroma of a just-sliced wedge, the overall beauty of the plant itself – especially when festooned with its glowing fruit during the darkest days of winter – how could one *not* be impressed with the 'Meyer' lemon?

So, in the tradition of Hokusai and Rivière, I'm offering 36 views of 'Meyer' lemons as companions to some very tasty recipes. As a subject to paint, they never cease to amaze me – appearing over and over again as gems of the plant kingdom, each its own bit of perfection from this garden state we call home.

Napa, California 2015

11

Frank Nicholas Meyer
1875 - 1918

I am pessimistic by nature, and have not found a road which leads to relaxation. I withdraw from humanity and try to find relaxation with plants. I live now in expectation of what will come.

Frank N. Meyer, from a 1901 letter to a friend

Considering the name "Meyer" occurs in the title of this book, it only seems fair that some consideration is given to the remarkable life of the man known as Frank N. Meyer who, considering his achievements, is pretty much unsung these days. Although there's not a great deal out there about his life, I came away with the impression that Meyer was not only a loner, but occasionally lonely, and for all the plants he found, I'm not sure he ever discovered another human being he could celebrate. Not to mention that this is a guy who had to keep his work boots on when he slept so the rats wouldn't chew on his ankles – but more about that later.

Thank Frank Nicholas Meyer for finding the 'Meyer' lemon in China (circa 1909) and introducing it to the West. One of his collecting bags can be seen, bottom right.

Born Frans Nicholaas Meijer in Amsterdam in 1875, Meyer showed an early interest in plants, beginning his horticultural career at age 14 working as a gardener's helper at the Amsterdam Botanical Garden. Encouraged by the director of the garden, Meyer became proficient in French and English and studied botany at the University of Groningen. A natural wanderer, Meyer left the botanic garden to see the plants and gardens of western Europe for himself, setting off on foot to travel through Belgium, Germany, France, Switzerland, Italy and Spain.

After his pedestrian tour of western Europe, Meyer traveled to England where he worked a stint in a commercial nursery before hitting the road again, this time to America. He arrived in 1901 and, with the help of his old boss at the Amsterdam Botanical Garden, got a job with the United States Department of Agriculture. After only a year, he was ready for adventure again and set off on his own to explore the indigenous plants of Mexico, Cuba, and California, working in nurseries along the way to pay for his expenses.

Three years later, Meyer returned to the USDA where he caught the eye of the chairman of the Foreign Plant Introduction Section, David Fairchild, who recognized Meyer's potential as an Agricultural Explorer, Meyer's official title. Fairchild introduced Meyer to Charles Sprague, the director of Harvard's Arnold Arboretum. Fairchild and Sprague worked out an arrangement for Meyer to study and collect plants in the Far East. Sprague was primarily interested in ornamental plants of commercial interest to America's nursery trade; Fairchild was more interested in food crops. Together they schooled Meyer in what had already been discovered so he wouldn't duplicate previous exploration efforts. With that they sent him off on a 13-year odyssey – four separate trips, each lasting 3 years or more – resulting in the introduction of approximately 2,500 species, including the 'Meyer' lemon.

In reading through Fairchild's and Sprague's correspondence with Meyer, I have to say they worked him like a rented mule. Their individual "wish lists" were as long as they were specific – everything from opium poppy seeds (anticipating the increased need for morphine with the outbreak of World War I), to soybeans (virtually unknown in America), water chestnuts (ditto), to lilacs, apricots, crabapples, Chinese pistachios and persimmons and everything in between. At one dark point in his travels, a doctor diagnoses Meyer as having "nervous prostration." Meyer wrote to Fairchild in 1917:

How long I myself will be able to travel about in China yet, I do not know, but it seems that I may return sooner than I expected, perhaps in 1918. The lone-

liness and the hardships of life here are beginning to be more and more distasteful to me and the time is approaching that I'll have to leave further exploration of China in the hands of younger men.

Fairchild, ever the task master, offers some weak tea in response:

If conditions stop your work you will of course cable me and we will arrange for your return to America. I hope they will allow you to go on exploring for we have only one life to live and we want to spend it enriching our own country with the plants of the world which produce good things to eat and to look at.

At various times, Meyer's journeys took him to Mongolia, Manchuria, Korea, Siberia, the Crimea, Azerbaijan, Armenia, Turkmenestan, Chinese Turkestan and Tibet, often during turbulent and dangerous political times when any foreigner was looked on with suspicion. Conditions were about as rough as can be imagined. In an April 16, 1917 letter to David Fairchild, Meyer makes one of his few complaints:

In the mountains whole villages are syphilitic; people without noses are often met with and syphilitic blindness and deafness are very common. In the inns the vermin are exceedingly plentiful and bloodthirsty and ordinary travelers have to sleep three abreast in one bedstead or on one broad bench and the stinkingly dirty bedcovers are kept in use until they fall to pieces. No wonder that 80% of the population suffers from all sorts of skin diseases, being inoculated by lice, fleas and bedbugs. I slept most times with my hunting boots on, for the vermin bites one especially at one's feet and legs, having learned no doubt that they are less easily caught there.

On his fourth and final expedition to the Far East in 1918, Meyer died aboard a steamer headed for Shanghai. The next day his body was found in the Yangtze River. Whether he fell from the steamer, either accidentally or on purpose, or was pushed, is not known. In the common parlance, it is written that he died under "mysterious circumstances." He was 43 years old. He is buried in Shanghai.

Our short life will never be long enough to find out all about this mighty land. When I think about all these unexplored areas, I get fairly dazzled; one will never be able to cover them all. I will have to roam around in my next life.

- Frank Meyer in a letter to David Fairchild, May, 1907

What's in a Name?

In 1909, when Frank Meyer encountered in China what would eventually become the 'Meyer' lemon, it appears that it was almost as much of a novelty to the Chinese as it was to Meyer himself. At the time, it was grown almost exclusively in containers, indoors and out, and enjoyed as the highly ornamental plant it is – the fruit being seen almost as an afterthought. Researchers are in general agreement that it was a naturally-occuring hybrid (rather than a man-made cross between two species) and even though most articles on 'Meyer' lemons state that it's a cross between the more standard sour lemon and a mandarin orange, genetic work done at the University of California at Riverside has shown that it is, in fact, a cross between a lemon and an orange. The defining characteristics of a 'Meyer' lemon are its thin skin, comparatively sweet flavor (less acidic than a sour lemon), extreme juiciness and an almost perfumelike fragrance. After it had been introduced to the American gardening public, it remained something of a backyard curiosity as opposed to a commercial crop, owing to the fact that its thin skin made it almost impossible to ship any distance. And so, for all of its charms, the 'Meyer' lemon languished in home gardens for generations, primarily in Florida, Texas and California. It wasn't until two culinary mavens, Alice Waters and Martha Stewart, started singing its praises that the 'Meyer' lemon finally received greater recognition and an almost cult status. With its new-found fame, the 'Meyer' lemon finally began showing up in grocery stores across the country during its rather short season of availability between between December and March, introducing a new generation to the pleasures of this unique citrus. Somewhere, Frank Meyer should be taking a well-deserved and long overdue bow.

In areas of the country too cold for the 'Meyer' lemon, it performs admirably well in containers indoors, just as it did when Frank Meyer originally found it in China more than 100 years ago.

15

Throughout the far west, Texas and Florida, 'Meyer' lemons are so ubiquitous in home gardens that they are almost taken for granted. What the rest of the country wouldn't give to have these delicious beauties right outside their back doors!

'MEYER' LIMONANA

There are lots of variations on this national drink of Israel and I'm here to put a further 'Meyer' twist on it. The first time I tried it, I was with my daughter in a middle eastern restaurant in Berkeley. She was an old hand at it; it was completely new to me – green, minty lemonade – who knew? It's not meant to be overly sweet, so the natural sweetness of the 'Meyer' lemon comes in handy here. If you're feeling particularly frisky, add a shot of gin or vodka to the mix. Serves two. L'chaim!

1 cup 'Meyer' lemon juice, approximately 7 or 8 lemons
½ cup roughly-torn or chopped fresh mint
1 cup water
4 tablespoons granulated sugar
2 cups ice cubes
Fresh mint sprigs for garnish

Put all ingredients in a blender and blend at high speed until the ice is well crushed. Serve in tall glasses, garnished with fresh mint sprigs.

Gardeners who have never grown 'Meyer' lemons before are astounded at the size of the crop these relatively small shrubs can produce. Luckily they last for months on the plants and can be harvested over time.

'MEYER' LEMON COOLER
WITH PROSECCO

Back in the day, some dubious liquor was marketed as "a lot to drink without drinking a lot." Well, this is just the opposite: light in every sense of the word, refreshing and non-fillling. A great hot weather drink, or when you're the designated driver.

Prosecco, well chilled
Club soda, cold
1 teaspoon 'Meyer' lemon juice
'Meyer' lemon peel, cut like a curled ribbon
Cracked ice

Fill a large, tall glass (a pilsner glass is best) with cracked ice. Pour the 'Meyer' lemon juice over the ice. Slowly fill the glass about two-thirds full with prosecco. Top with the club soda and give it a quick stir. Rub the rim of the glass with the 'Meyer' lemon ribbon and leave as a garnish.

I purchased this cocktail shaker from the estate of Laurence Sickman, long-time Curator of Oriental Art at the Nelson-Atkins Museum in Kansas City, where he assembled one of the great collections of Asian art in the world. Made in China of Chinese silver, it seems right at home with Frank Meyer's lemons.

PORTUGUESE SCOTCH SOUR

Way back when, sometime in the 1970s when Whiskey Sours were far more popular than they are now, a sophisticated friend of mine introduced me to this drink. She had spent time in Portugal and told me they were all the rage there. True or not, this is a delicious drink, especially if you're a Scotch drinker. Perfect during hot weather, but watch out: they go down so easy you may find yourself being taken home in a wheelbarrow.

2 ounces Scotch whisky
Juice of ½ 'Meyer' lemon
1 teaspoon superfine sugar
Mint sprig for garnish, if desired

Put whisky, lemon juice and sugar in a cocktail shaker about half filled with ice cubes. Shake vigorously. Strain into a chilled cocktail glass. Garnish with a sprig of mint. Fasten your seatbelt …

Having the right glass for a particular drink may be going the way of the dodo bird, but way back when, it would have been unthinkable to serve a Tom Collins in anything other than a "Collins glass."

'MEYER' LEMON TOM COLLINS

Although the traditional Tom Collins cocktail is made with gin, as you can see in the illustration, I prefer mine made with vodka. Pick your poison, as they say. The nice thing about building your own Tom Collins is that you can adjust the sweetness to your own preference; for me, the less sweet it is, the more refreshing its effect. It has been popular since the mid-1800s, when it was described as "gin and sparkling lemonade," which is exactly what it is. A "Collins glass" is one which is taller and narrower than a standard highball glass and is considered de rigueur for serving this classic cocktail.

2 ounces vodka (or gin)
1 teaspoon superfine sugar
½ ounce 'Meyer' lemon juice
Club soda
Thin lemon wedge
Sprig of fresh mint

Combine vodka, sugar and lemon juice in a Collins glass ¾ full of cracked ice. Stir briefly, top with club soda or seltzer, garnish with lemon slice and spring of mint and serve with a stirring rod.

It really is as if 'Meyer' lemons are filled with sunshine, glowing from within — at least that was my intent with this painting.

'MEYER' LEMON LIMONCELLO

Bright and refreshing, limoncello is wonderful as a palate cleanser, especially as an after-dinner drink served icy-cold, straight, in a chilled shot glass. It is an incomparable digestive; mixed with tonic water it is a sweet, tasty refreshment. It's also great with champagne or mixed with juice as a cocktail. This recipe is courtesy of Everclear – yes, that very high octane liquor more commonly known as "white lightning." That said, they know a thing or two about making an excellent limoncello.

10 'Meyer' lemons, peels only
1 (750-ml) bottle Everclear
3½ cups water
2½ cups granulated sugar

Using a vegetable peeler, peel 10 freshly washed, organic lemons, leaving as much of the white pith behind as possible. If there's pith still left on the peels, lay them peel side down and scrape the pith away using a sharp paring knife. If left on, the pith will cause the limoncello to be bitter.

Combine lemon zest and Everclear in a large, sealable container, at least 2 quarts in size. Let steep for at least 4 days and up to 4 weeks in a cool, dry place.

After the lemon-Everclear mixture is infused to your liking, combine sugar and water in a medium saucepan. Bring to a boil, stirring regularly until sugar is fully dissolved, approximately 5-10 minutes. Let syrup cool to room temperature. Add the simple syrup to the lemon infusion gradually, tasting as you go, until it has the level of sweetness you desire.

Strain mixture through a fine mesh stainer. Pour into smaller bottles and chill in freezer. Enjoy.

It continues to amaze me that 'Meyer' lemons are at the absolute height of their glory in the darkest days of winter. Their beauty, fragrance and flavor brighten many a gloomy winter day.

26

'MEYER' LEMON
INFUSED OLIVE OIL

This is so easy, it's a shame more people don't make lemon-infused olive oil. I bought an 8.5-ounce bottle of 'Meyer' lemon-infused olive oil for $12. I made a similar amount at home and taste-tested them, side-by-side, and couldn't tell the difference. The homemade version cost a little over $1. Once you have it on hand, you'll find yourself using it instead of regular olive oil all the time. It's particularly good in vinaigrettes on fresh green salads. Even better on a classic mozzarella and tomato Caprese salad.

1 large 'Meyer' lemon, or 2 small ones
1 cup olive oil

Wash the lemon under running water and dry thoroughly. Using a vegetable peeler or sharp paring knife, cut the zest from the lemon in strips. You only want the yellow part – not the rather bitter white pith below.

Put lemon zest and olive oil in a small sauce pan and warm over low heat. Do not allow oil to simmer. Keep the oil just below a simmer for about 10 minutes. Remove oil from heat and let cool.

Strain out lemon zest and pour the infused oil into a clean bottle or jar. Store in a cool, dark place.

Preserved 'Meyer' lemons are so easy to prepare – and such an important and distinctive addition to so many dishes – you owe it to yourself to make some right away. French Hermitique jars, with their tight rubber seals, are ideal containers for this exotic treat. Preserved lemons last practically forever if kept in the refrigerator.

MOROCCAN PRESERVED 'MEYER' LEMONS

As exotic as Moroccan perserved lemons sounds, they are very easy to make at home. If you have a bumper crop, as so many people do, make several jars and give as special gifts. Nothing else tastes quite like preserved 'Meyer' lemons; once you start using them, you'll be hooked. Be advised they are very salty; most people lightly rinse them in cold water and blot them dry before using. Most recipes use the rind only, not the flesh.

6 to 7 'Meyer' lemons
¼ cup kosher or sea salt
8 black peppercorns
1 bay leaf
1 whole dried red pepper (optional)
Extra lemons for juice

1 sterilized half-liter jar

Put one tablespoon of the salt into the bottom of the jar. Cut the lemons into quarters, from the top down, leaving the bottom ½ inch of the lemon still joined as one. Sprinkle salt on the exposed flesh and press into lemons. Pack the lemons tightly into the jar, adding the peppercorns, bay leaf, and red pepper (if desired) as you go, and more salt evenly between layers. If the juice produced by packing them into the jar isn't enough to cover them, add more lemon juice until they are submerged. Leave a little airspace at the top and seal the jar.

Store the jar at room temperature for 30 days, shaking the jar occasionally. After 30 days, store the preserved lemons in the refrigerator.

'Meyer' lemons on the bush – in bud, flower, and fruit. Somewhat surprisingly, 'Meyer' lemons hold exceptionally well on the plant, sometimes up to a year.

RHUBARB LEMON CHUTNEY

One of my mother's favorites, adapted from an old Ball Canning recipe. The inclusion of rhubarb made it fairly novel – for a while, at least. It was a perennial addition to our Thanksgiving Day feast. Truth be told, with all the other flavors going on here, the 'Meyer' lemon does not exactly shine. All the same, we were always looking for ways to use our sizeable crop.

10 whole black peppercorns
1 tablespoon mustard seeds
1 tablespoon pickling spice
2 tablespoons grated orange zest
⅓ cup fresh orange juice
2 tablespoons grated 'Meyer' lemon zest
⅓ cup fresh 'Meyer' lemon juice
6 cups chopped rhubarb
5 cups lightly-packed brown sugar
3½ cups cider vinegar
3 cups chopped red onion
1½ cups raisins
2 tablespoons finely-chopped garlic
2 tablespoons finely-chopped gingerroot
1 tablespoon curry powder
1 teaspoon ground allspice

Tie peppercorns, mustard seeds and pickling spice in a square of cheese-cloth, creating a spice bag. Set aside.

Combine orange and lemon zest and juice, rhubarb, brown sugar, vinegar, onions, raisins, garlic, and ginger in a large stainless steel saucepan. Bring to a boil over medium-high heat, stirring constantly. Reduce heat and boil gently, stirring occasionally, for 45 minutes. Add curry powder, allspice, and reserved spice bag; stir well. Boil gently, stirring frequently, until thick enough to mound on spoon, about 30 minutes.

Allow to cool. Pour into six sterilized half pint canning jars. Process according to jar manufacturer instructions.

Even bringing just one 'Meyer' lemon into your kitchen and cutting into it is quite the sensory experience – pleasing the eyes, the nose and your taste buds.

'MEYER' LEMON MARMALADE

My friend, Patty, who has a giant 'Meyer' lemon bush right outside her kitchen window, came up with this recipe. It's the essence of simplicity and delicious, just as it is. The late Nan McEvoy, founder of the McEvoy Ranch in Petaluma (known for its world-class olive oils), suggested combining 'Meyer' lemon marmalade with soy sauce as glaze for broiled salmon. Sounds good it me!

4 'Meyer' lemons, very thinly sliced, seeds removed
4 cups water
4 cups granulated sugar

After the lemons have been thinly sliced and deseeded, roughly chop. You should have about two cups. Put four cups of water in a heavy sauce pan over medium-high heat. Bring to a boil and add the chopped lemons. Boil gently for 30 to 40 minutes, until the chopped lemons have softened. Add the sugar and increase heat under the pan. Bring mixture to a boil, stirring constantly, until the mixture has reached 220ºF degrees on a candy thermometer.

Allow to cool slightly and then pour into sterilized jars. Marmalade can be processed in a hot water bath, according to the canning jar manufacturer's instructions, or simply refrigerated.

Vintage fruit box labels often employed a fair amount of fantasy in their landscape depictions, but there are actually places in California that look like this.

CANDIED 'MEYER' LEMON PEEL

Like Moroccan Preserved Lemons (page 29), candied 'Meyer' lemon peels are easy to make and very versatile – dip them in melted chocolate, put in any muffin, bread, cake or cookie recipe, or add as topping on ice cream. You get the idea.

4 'Meyer' lemons, peels only
2 cups sugar, divided
1 cup water

Using a vegetable peeler, peel four freshly washed 'Meyer' lemons, leaving as much of the white pith behind as possible. If there's pith still left on the peels, lay them peel side down and scrape the pith away using a sharp paring knife. If left on, the pith will cause the candied peels to be bitter.

Put strips of lemon zest, 1 cup of the sugar, and 1 cup of water in a medium saucepan and bring to a boil. Reduce heat and simmer gently until peels are translucent, about 10 minutes.

Drain peels in a colander for an hour or so, shaking occasionally to remove as much of the syrup as possible.

Lay the peels in a single layer on cooling racks for at least an hour or up to overnight.

Put remaining cup of sugar in a wide bowl or large rimmed plate. Toss the peels in the sugar, a handful at a time, to coat each strip of peel thoroughly. Lay sugared strips back on the cooling racks. Let dry for 5 to 6 hours. They can be eaten, or used in baking recipes, as is, but should be used in a day or two. For longer storage, set racks in a 180°-200°F oven for an hour or so to dry them more thoroughly. Dried this way, the candied peel can be kept in an airtight container for up to a month.

This is what 'Meyer' lemons look like in autumn, before they ripen in time for the winter holidays. I thought of calling this "Fifty Shades of Green," but thought better of it.

'MEYER' LEMON GREMOLATA

From Italy, gremolata is a finely-chopped combination of fresh parsley, lemon zest and garlic. Traditionally, it is sprinkled on rich, braised meats (such as ossobucco) just before serving. It adds some high, fresh notes which most folks believe complement the unctuousness of slow-cooked meats. Others think it's gilding the lily. Personally I love what it does and would put it on breakfast cereal if I could get away with it. The unique flavor and aroma of 'Meyer' lemons, not to mention the tangerine, makes this a distinctive version of gremolata.

1 'Meyer' lemon, peel only
1 tangerine
2 to 3 cloves of garlic
Large handful of fresh curly parsley

Wash the 'Meyer' lemon and tangerine under running water and dry. Using a vegetable peeler, peel the lemon, leaving as much of the white pith behind as possible. The tangerine will be easy to peel by hand. If there's pith still left on any of the peels, lay them peel side down and scrape the pith away using a sharp paring knife. If left on, the pith will cause the gremolata to be bitter.

Put the peels, garlic cloves, and parsley into a pile and chop until all the ingredients are the same small size. Use immediately as a garnish on braised meats, pasta, or fish.

*This is a Japanse bowl from my father, with a landscape scene painted on
the outside on a white background; the inside, however, is this amazing
turquoise, a great complement to the intense yellow-gold of the lemons.*

PRESERVED LEMON & TOMATO SALAD

This salad has a distinctly Mediterranean feel to it. Personally, when I've been making salads recently, I find myself using far less lettuce and far more vegetables instead. With some experimentation, you can come up with some delicious (healthful!) combinations. This one's a winner.

4 large, ripe tomatoes, deseeded, cut into 1-inch chunks
1 small red onion, thinly sliced and chopped
1 bunch radishes, thinly sliced
1 large carrot, peeled and grated
½ cup feta cheese, crumbled
½ preserved lemon, peel only, lightly rinsed, blotted dry and diced
3 tablespoons olive oil
Juice of ½ 'Meyer' lemon
1 large handful fresh parsley, finely chopped
1 large handful fresh mint, finely chopped

Place the tomatoes, onions, radishes, and shredded carrots into a large shallow bowl. Make a quick dressing by combining the preserved lemon, olive oil and lemon juice and mixing with a fork. Drizzle dressing over the salad ingredients. Top with the crumbled feta, chopped parsley and mint and toss lightly. Serve with warm crusty bread.

Somewhat amazingly, 'Meyer' lemons are content to spend their entire lives growing in containers. This is especially convenient when growing them in cold winter climates, where the plants can be moved under protection for the winter.

AMY'S 'MEYER' SALSA

I love my friend Amy's cooking. Her 'Meyer' lemon chicken is featured on page 69. Her style is a full-flavored one and this recipe is no exception. Excellent on grilled fish or chicken.

1 'Meyer' lemon
¼ cup shallot, minced
1½ tablespoons sherry vinegar
¼ cup finely-chopped curly parsley
2 tablespoons chives, finely chopped
⅓ cup extra-virgin olive oil
Kosher salt, to taste
Freshly ground pepper, to taste

Slice the lemons, including peel, as thinly as possible. Remove seeds. Chop the lemon slices into a small dice. Combine the diced lemons with the rest of the ingredients in a medium bowl. Stir to combine. Let stand 30 minutes for flavors to "marry." Will keep for several days, covered, in the refrigerator.

My friend Kathy Kearns, owner of Crockett Pottery (www.crockettpottery.com), has absolutely mastered the cobalt blue glaze, a perfect contrast to the intense color of the 'Meyer' lemon.

NAPA CABBAGE
'MEYER' LEMON SLAW

I'm not sure how this variation of coleslaw came into being, but I'm sure glad it did! I've never been a big fan of slaw until I started making it with Napa cabbage. I really like its softer texture and the almost complete lack of sulphur odor so characteristic of most cabbages. Since I was starting with an Asian vein, I just kept with it, resulting in this "not your grandmother's coleslaw."

3 cups Napa cabbage, shredded
4 chopped green onions, white and green parts
⅓ cup fresh cilantro, chopped
1 small carrot, shredded
1 fresh jalapeño chile, seeds removed, diced (optional)
1 tablespoon toasted sesame seeds
Juice of one 'Meyer' lemon
1½ teaspoons mirin (substitute granulated sugar if you don't have
    mirin)
1 tablespoon toasted sesame oil
2 tablespoons rice wine vinegar

Place the shredded cabbage, green onions, cilantro, shredded carrots, optional jalapeño chiles and toasted sesame seeds in a large bowl. Toss lightly. Make the dressing by combining lemon juice, mirin, toasted sesame oil and rice vinegar in a small bowl, whisking it with a fork. Pour over the slaw ingredients and toss thoroughly. Refrigerate for 30 minutes or so to allow the flavors to "marry." Be prepared to like slaw, even if you never have before.

This is one of my grandfather's ginger jars (see page 87), dating back to the 1920s. Yes, it really was filled with large pieces of ginger root, preserved in a thick sugar syrup. Pretty exotic when I was a kid.

CRISPY NEW POTATOES WITH MISO 'MEYER' MAYONNAISE

I'm not going to enter the fray as to whether or not it was the Belgians or the French who invented "French fries," but I know from firsthand experience that Belgians love the combination of French fries and mayonnaise. This dish was inspired by one I ran across on Food 52, the excellent food blog found on the internets machine. I tweaked it a bit and I'm here to tell you it's some kind of wonderful. Try them once and I guarantee they'll become a favorite.

1½ pounds new potatoes
¼ cup mayonnaise
2 teaspoons miso paste (brown is best)
Juice of ½ 'Meyer' lemon; zest from one 'Meyer' lemon
Oil for frying (olive oil preferred)
2 stalks of green onions, trimmed and thinly sliced

Scrub the potatoes and place on a steamer in a pot with a lid. It's okay to stack them on top of each other. Bring water to a boil, cover pot, and reduce to a simmer. Start checking potatoes after 8 minutes. They're done when the tip of sharp knife penetrates to the center of the potato easily.

While the potatoes cook, spray or wipe a large platter with oil. Spread the cooked potatoes on the platter; let them sit for 5 minutes to cool slightly.

Mix the mayonnaise, miso, and lemon juice and zest thoroughly in a small bowl. Store in refrigerator until ready to use.

When the potatoes are cool enough to touch, gently smash/flatten them with the heel of your hand. Try to keep them whole.

In a skillet, fry the potatoes in about ¼ inch of oil over medium-high heat until the edges start to brown, about 2 minutes per side. Place cooked potatoes on a sheet pan lined with newspaper, a grocery bag, or paper towels. When you're done frying them, place on a platter and top with green onions, then serve immediately with the miso mayonnaise. Serves 4.

About halfway through this painting I began to wonder what I had gotten myself into . . .

MOROCCAN AVOCADO TOAST AND POACHED EGGS

The older I get, the more I seem to gravitate to simple dishes with a handful of ingredients. This one definitely qualifies, not only for its simplicity, but its memorable flavors. Surprisingly rich, one egg-topped slice of avocado toast may be enough for all but the biggest eaters.

1 ripe avocado, halved and pitted
¼ preserved lemon, rind only, lightly rinsed and diced, plus a little curing liquid, if desired
2 slices sourdough bread
2 eggs
Pinch salt
Jalapeño or serrano peppers, finely diced, or Aleppo pepper, or good-quality harissa as an accompaniment, if desired

Scoop avocado flesh into a bowl. Dice the cured lemon and add it to the avocado. Mash lightly with a fork. Taste for seasoning; add a drizzle of curing liquid, if desired, plus a sprinkle of salt. Toast your bread the way you like it. While the bread is toasting, poach two eggs. When they reach your desired donenesss, remove from water, place on a couple of layers of paper towel to remove excess water. Spread avocado mixture on the bread, then top with eggs. Sprinkle eggs with finely diced jalapeño or serrano peppers, Aleppo pepper, or harissa. Breakfast is served!

A friend took a look at this painting and said "too bad you can't smell it."
She was right: the fragrance of 'Meyer' lemon blossoms is heavenly.

PASTA with DANDELION GREENS, PRESERVED LEMON and TOASTED WALNUTS

I admit that whole wheat pasta is a little rustic, even for this old hippie. But there's something wonderful about the combination of whole wheat pasta, slightly bitter greens, 'Meyer' lemons and toasted walnuts. It's a classic winter dish if there ever was one and is, of course, really good for you. If you've never tried dandelion greens, do. They are at the top of my list of all things green. I know that tradition dictates that two ounces of dry pasta is considered a single serving, but that may be a little shy if it's being served as a main course. That said, following tradition, this recipe serves two; doubles easily for four.

4 ounces whole wheat pasta, linguine or spaghetti
1 bunch dandelion greens
½ cup part skim Ricotta cheese
3 tablespoons 'Meyer' lemon-infused olive oil (page 25), plus more
   for drizzling over the top
½ cup toasted, chopped walnuts, lightly salted
2 to 4 tablespoons grated Parmesan-Reggiano cheese
Zest of one 'Meyer' lemon

Cook the pasta according to package directions. Drain and toss with 1 tablespoon of the lemon-infused olive oil. Reserve. Place a large skillet over medium-high heat. Add 1 tablespoon of the infused oil to the pan. Rough cut the dandelion greens and add to the skillet. Sauté for a couple of minutes until they're just shy of being completely wilted. Set aside. In a bowl, mix the last tablespoon of infused oil and lemon zest to the ricotta cheese; mix thoroughly. Place the pan with the wilted greens over medium-high heat. Add the ricotta mixture and stir to mix. Add the pasta and toss to evenly distribute the ricotta and greens. Place the pasta in warmed, wide shallow bowls. Garnish with the toasted walnuts and Parmesan cheese.

I was very complimented when a friend of mine – who happens to be a very fine artist – purchased this painting for his private collection.

'MEYER' LEMON SCAMPI
on SPAGHETTI

This dish comes together very quickly. Aficionados of all things Italian may take issue with the combination of shrimp and pasta, but I say it's a flavorful, satisfying combination. It's easy enough for a weeknight meal, but special enough for a dinner party. Serve with crusty bread and a green salad.

1 pound spaghetti
1 tablespoon olive oil
2 large shallots, finely chopped
½ red bell pepper, seeded and diced
3 to 4 cloves garlic, minced or pressed
Two 8-ounce bottles clam juice
¼ cup dry vermouth
½ cup curly parsley, finely chopped
Juice and zest of 2 large 'Meyer' lemons
Freshly ground black pepper, to taste
Kosher salt, to taste
1 pound medium prawns, uncooked, peeled and deveined (20 to 25 per pound)

Bring a large pot of salted water to a boil. Add the spaghetti and cook according to package instructions. When done, drain, do not rinse, and return to pot. Toss with 1 tablespoon olive oil. Set aside until sauce is finished.

While pasta is cooking, add additional 1 tablespoon olive oil to a large sauté pan over medium-high heat. Add shallots, red bell pepper, garlic, and lemon zest. Sauté until just wilted.

Add the clam juice, dry vermouth, parsley, lemon juice, black pepper and salt to the pan. Bring to a boil and add the prawns, all at once. Stir rapidly. The prawns will be done as soon as they turn pink, 2 to 3 minutes. Do not be tempted to cook longer as the prawns will become tough.

Put the drained pasta in a large bowl with low sides. Pour the sauce over the pasta and serve it forth.

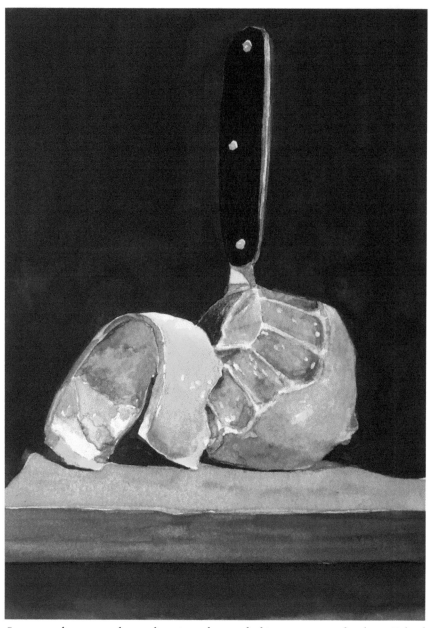

It seems that several people misunderstood this painting, thinking I had stabbed the lemon. Not so: my pocketknife is stuck into the cutting board, not *the lemon.*

SCALLOPS on TOASTED CORNBREAD
with 'MEYER' SABAYON SAUCE

The idea for this dish came to me while visiting a friend on the coast of Connecticut. It was summer and the fresh corn was plentiful – so plentiful that we were able to experiment with several different takes on chowder. My favorite was one which combined corn kernels and scallops and which gradually morphed into this recipe, the flavors of which can only be described as "sexy." Really. You can make your own cornbread, but I use the boxed Jiffy Cornbread Mix; even some of my southern friends say they can't make it any better than Jiffy. Serves two.

1 package Jiffy Cornbread Mix (for which you will need ⅓ cup milk and 1 egg)
6 to 8 sea scallops (3 to 4 per diner)
1 tablespoon butter
½ red pepper, diced
1 large shallot, diced
2 tablespoons fresh parsley, finely chopped
½ cup frozen corn kernels, thawed (fire-roasted, if possible)
Softened butter for cornbread

For the sauce:
¼ cup heavy cream
4 large egg yolks
2 tablespoons 'Meyer' lemon juice
Zest from one-half 'Meyer' lemon
½ teaspoon salt

Make the cornbread, according to package directions, in an 8 by 8 inch baking pan. The "loaf" will be very thin, but just right for this dish.

Melt the butter in a skillet; add red pepper, shallot, parsley and corn kernels. Sauté until just wilted; 2 to 3 minutes. Remove from skillet and set aside. Remove the skillet from the heat, but do not wipe it out; you'll be using it later, as is, for the scallops.

Continued on page 88

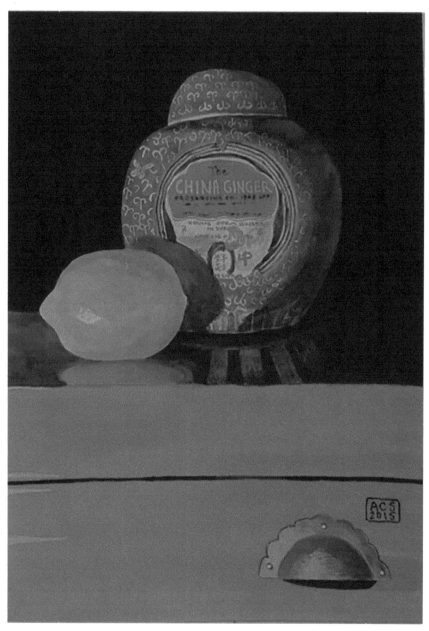

I recently unearthed this ginger jar from some random box in my garage. It hadn't been touched since the 1960s – complete with its tattered paper label and the ginger in sugar syrup still inside!

FISH & CHIPS with 'MEYER' CRISPS

Some things just don't work out: This recipe started as a Japanese take on fish and chips, using calamari steaks, tempura batter and slices of fried 'Meyer' lemons. Like I said, some things just don't work out. What evolved is the easiest and best batter for fish and chips ever. The fried slices of 'Meyer' lemon stayed because they were very tasty and a great complement to the fish. Serve with Napa Cabbage 'Meyer' Lemon Slaw, page 43. Serves 4.

For the batter:
One (12-ounce) bottle beer
2 cups all-purpose flour
Kosher salt, to taste
Freshly ground pepper, to taste

1½ pounds cod fillets, skinned, bones removed, cut into 2- or 3-inch
    chunks
1 to 2 'Meyer' lemons, cut into thin slices
Your favorite frozen French fries
Plenty of 'Meyer' lemon wedges for squeezing

Preheat oven to 225ºF.
In a heavy skillet, heat at least one inch of vegetable oil to 375ºF. Slice the lemons and reserve.

In a large bowl, mix the flour, salt, pepper and beer until you have a smooth batter. Place fish chunks on several layers of paper towels and pat dry.

Start by coating the lemon slices in the batter and slide into the hot oil. Flip as they begin to brown, about 2 minutes total. Transfer to a paper towel-lined baking sheet and keep warm in oven.

Fry the French fries according to package instructions. Keep warm in oven.

Season fish on both sides with salt and pepper. Coat them completely with the batter. Gently add to the hot oil. Fry fish until deep golden and cooked through, 4 to 5 minutes. Transfer to oven. Serve with plenty of lemon wedges.

A French drying cloth, with its cobalt blue stripe, seemed like the perfect contrasting partner for this pair of 'Meyer' lemons, all reflected in the silver julep cup.

'MEYER' LEMON CRAB LOUIS

This is my go-to hot weather dish. Beautiful to look at and delicious to eat. Served with warm, rustic French bread, this is substantial enough to be a main dish. If Dungeness crab is not available, bay shrimp also works well. Serves 4.

1½ pounds crab meat, preferably Dungeness
¼ cup 'Meyer' lemon juice
2 teaspoons grated 'Meyer' lemon zest
1 large head butter lettuce (reserve four of the biggest outside leaves)
Cherry tomatoes, cut in half
Cucumber slices
Green onions, sliced, both white and green parts
Red pepper, diced
Hearts of palm, chilled, cut into quarters, lengthwise
4 hard-boiled eggs, cut into quarters
8 'Meyer' lemon wedges

For dressing:
1 cup mayonnaise
¼ cup Sriracha or ketchup-based chili sauce
1 teaspoon grated 'Meyer' lemon zest

Mix the mayonnaise, Sriracha sauce and lemon zest in a bowl. The amount of Sriracha sauce can be adjusted up or down, depending on your taste. Reserve in refrigerator.

In a large bowl, toss crab meat with lemon juice and zest. Keep in refrigerator until ready to use. Rinse and blot dry four, large, whole butter leaves and place one on each individual plate. Rough cut the remaining lettuce and divide equally on top of the four whole lettuce leaves. Arrange the tomatoes, cucumbers, hearts of palm, lemon wedges and hard-boiled eggs on the perimeter of the lettuce. Add the dressed crab meat in the middle of the lettuce, in a neat pile. Scatter the green onions and diced red peppers over all and pass the dressing. Good eating!

A bowl full of practically luminescent 'Meyer' lemons, along with a couple of their distant cousins, the 'Bearss' lime.

SNAPPY SALMON

This dish goes together very quickly – fast enough for a weeknight meal, tasty enough for dinner-party fare. Inspired by a recipe from the excellent food blog, Food52 *(https://food52.com) which, in turn, was inspired from Sommer Collier's blog, A Spicy Perspective. I've modified it a bit further, but the basic idea remains the same: Using a microplane zester/grater, grate fresh garlic cloves, a jalapeño chile, and zest a 'Meyer' lemon. Mix the grated ingredients together with a little olive oil, spread on the salmon and cook. Good, fresh flavors to complement good, fresh fish! Feel free to adjust the amounts jalapeño, garlic, and lemon to suit your taste. Serves 4.*

1½ pounds salmon fillets or steaks, approximately 6 ounces each and
    1-inch thick
2 tablespoons olive oil
1 'Meyer' lemon, zest and juice (divided)
2 garlic cloves, minced
1 fresh jalapeño chile
Salt and freshly ground pepper, to taste

Grate/zest the lemon, garlic cloves and chile and place in a small bowl. Add the olive oil and juice of one-half of the lemon; mix thoroughly. Set aside.

Arrange the salmon in a single layer on a plate. Pat dry with a paper towel. Salt and pepper to taste. Pour the lemon-garlic-chile mixture evenly over the salmon. Let sit for 10 minutes or so.

Heat a medium-sized skillet, lightly oiled, on medium-high for three minutes or so. Add the salmon to the hot pan and sear the skin-side for four to five minutes – until browned and crispy – then flip. Sear the flesh side for three to four minutes, or until golden brown. This will cook the salmon to about medium. If you like your salmon softer and less cooked, use an instant-read thermometer and remove when it reaches 125° F. That said, the USDA recommends cooking salmon to 145°F. Squeeze the remaining half lemon over the top and serve hot.

Alberta Binford and William McCloskey were husband and wife American painters in the late 19th and early 20th century. Amongst other subjects, they became famous for their amazing depictions of tissue-wrapped citrus. This is my homage to their beautiful work.

CONFIT OF TUNA

Inspired by a recipe that originally appeared in The New York Times, *this dish is the real deal. Absolutely delicious as part of an antipasto platter, tossed with pasta, or in a Salade Niçoise.*

1 pound tuna (albacore or yellowfin), fresh or thawed frozen, 1-inch thick, cut into 1-inch cubes
1 teaspoon Kosher or sea salt
½ teaspoon crushed red pepper flakes
2 tablespoons thinly-sliced garlic
Freshly ground black pepper, to taste
1 bay leaf
Zest and juice of one-half 'Meyer' lemon
1 tablespoon capers, drained
1 cup olive oil, plus more if necessary

Trim any skin, bones or dark blood spots from the tuna and discard. Place the cubes of tuna in a 1-quart saucepan (if the pan is too big, you'll use too much olive oil – the cubes should fit snugly in the pan). Add the salt, red pepper flakes, garlic and black pepper and stir gently to distribute seasonings evenly. Add the bay leaf and lemon zest and lemon juice and pour enough olive oil to just barely cover the fish. It will be about 1 cup, though you may need a little more for topping off.

Place the saucepan over very low heat; the oil may get hot enough that a few bubbles rise from the bottom, but it should not simmer. Cook until the tuna just begins to flake, about 15 minutes.

Let the tuna cool to warm room temperature before transferring to a storage container. If you're going to use the tuna the same day, refrigeration is not necessary. The tuna will keep, tightly sealed and refrigerated, for at least a week, but not more than 10 days. Warm to room temperature before using. Just excellent!

For whatever reason, I find it almost impossible to paint anywhere other than my kitchen table. Go figure. The windows face south and east, resulting in some very strong sunshine – and equally strong shadow patterns – across the table.

GRILLED OYSTERS WITH 'MEYER' LEMON-GARLIC SAUCE

Oysters are the easiest of the bivalves to cook directly over a fire. Although large oysters may be shucked, drained, and cooked on skewers (where they will shrink considerably, an advantage if the oysters are especially large), it's far easier to simply cook unopened oysters which, seemingly by magic, open by themselves. Make sure to place them on the grill flat shell up, so the bottom, cupped shell can hold the oyster "liquor" and garlicky lemon butter sauce.

24 large oysters in their shells
1 cup butter
4 large garlic cloves, pressed
Juice and zest of one lemon
Tabasco or other hot sauce to taste

Scrub the oysters well and store them, flat shell up, in a shallow pan or bucket until ready to cook. Cover with a damp towel or burlap; do not store in water.

Prepare a hot fire in an open grill.

Combine the butter, garlic, lemon juice, and hot sauce in a saucepan. Simmer over low heat while the oysters are on the grill.

Place the oysters directly over a hot fire, flat shell up. Have a pair of oven mitts and an oyster knife at the ready. As soon as the oyster shells pop open, remove them from fire, and open them completely with the oyster knife, discarding the top shell. Add a spoonful of the butter sauce to each oyster and put back on the grill until the liquid is bubbly and the oyster begins to shrink and curl at the edge.

Serve immediately. In all truthfulness, the oysters probably won't even make it to a serving platter: True oyster lovers are content to hover around the grill, popping them in their mouths as soon as they come off the fire!

The best part of the day: chicken on the grill, shadows lengthening, adult beverage close-at-hand and a 'Meyer' lemon bush laden with fruit, right at the doorstep.

GRILLED HALIBUT WITH 'MEYER' LEMON-GREEN OLIVE SAUCE

Fresh halibut is one of the finest fish there is for grilling: delicate, sweet, and moist. Unfortunately, the process of freezing and thawing halibut robs it of most of its moisture and delicacy, so stick to the fresh form if at all possible. The lemon-green olive sauce elevates this dish into the "special" category. Serves 4.

For the sauce:
1 large shallot, finely diced
¼ cup fresh parsley, finely chopped
3 tablespoons 'Meyer' lemon juice
1 tablespoon 'Meyer' lemon zest
½ preserved lemon, peel only, finely chopped
1 serrano chile, seeded and finely diced
1 cup tomato, finely chopped (small yellow pear tomatoes are preferred)
8 pimiento-filled green olives, sliced

For the fish:
4 halibut steaks, about 1½ to 2 pounds total, each about 1-inch thick
Vegetable oil
Paprika
Ground white pepper

To make the lemon-green olive sauce, combine all the ingredients in a bowl and mix well. Allow to sit for at least 30 minutes to allow flavors to meld.

Rub a little vegetable oil onto both sides of each halibut steak and then dust with paprika and white pepper.

Once the grill is hot (you should be able to hold you hand one inch above the grill and just spell "Mississippi"), and cook the halibut for about 4 to 5 minutes per side, turning it once. The fish is done when it just begins to flake when probed with a fork.

Serve hot off the grill with a generous dollop of the lemon-green olive sauce on top.

More bright morning light streaming in across my kitchen table, made even brighter with the offering of 'Meyer' lemons.

SEA BASS with 'MEYER' LEMON BEURRE BLANC

It's not my intent to go all Old School on you with this recipe because, actually, I rarely cook this way anymore. There are times, however, when nothing but the real McCoy will do. Delicate in flavor and texture, sea bass is beautifully complemented by the tangy richness of the beurre blanc sauce. With the aid of a Thermos bottle, pre-heated with hot water, the beurre blanc can be made well before you grill the fish. Serves 4.

For the beurre blanc:
3 to 4 shallots, finely diced
¼ cup white wine vinegar
¼ cup white wine
Juice and zest of ½ 'Meyer' lemon
1 cup (2 sticks) unsalted butter, cut into about 10 pats

4 sea bass fillets, approximately 6 ounces each
Vegetable oil
White pepper

To make the beurre blanc, combine the shallots, vinegar, wine, and lemon juice and zest in a small saucepan and bring to a boil. Watch carefully and stir or swirl the mixture more or less constantly. Continue to boil rapidly until only 2 tablespoons of liquid remain. Reduce the heat to medium-low and begin adding the butter, one pat at a time, whisking constantly. Allow each pat of butter to dissolve almost completely before adding the next. By the time the last pat of butter has been added, the sauce should be thick and creamy. Pour the sauce into a preheated Thermos bottle to hold until serving time.

Rinse the sea bass fillets under cold running water and blot dry with paper towels. Rub a little vegetable oil on both sides of each fillet, then dust with white pepper. Place the sea bass on a hot grill and cook until they just begin to flake when probed with a fork, 4 to 5 minutes per side, turning them once. To serve, pour a few tablespoons of the beurre blanc over each fillet and garnish with and a little parsley, if desired.

It continues to amaze me that 'Meyer' lemons are at the absolute height of their glory in the darkest days of winter. Their beauty, fragrance, and flavor brighten many a gloomy winter day.

AMY'S ROAST 'MEYER' CHICKEN

Amy is a good friend of mine and one of the best cooks I know. Her dishes all have a distinctive California flare and this 'Meyer' lemon chicken is no exception. Good eating! Amy roasts hers in the oven; I prefer doing it on my trusty Weber charcoal grill, using the indirect method, with the coals on one side of the grate and the chicken on the other side of the grill, lid on, vent holes positioned over the chicken.

1 whole chicken, 3½ to 4 pounds
5 large 'Meyer' lemons
Kosher or sea salt, to taste
Freshly ground black pepper, to taste
4 or 5 large sprigs fresh rosemary
1 large head garlic, individual cloves smashed and peeled
2 tablespoons butter, softened

Preheat oven to 425°F. Fold the wing tips under the back of the chicken, and place in a roasting pan not much larger than the chicken. Juice the lemons and pour over the chicken and inside the cavity. Generously salt and pepper the chicken inside and out. Make a bed of three sprigs of rosemary under the chicken and place one or two sprigs inside the cavity. Break the garlic head into cloves, smash them with the side of a knife and discard peels; and add a few to the cavity and the rest to the pan around the chicken. Rub the softened butter across the breasts and tops of drumsticks.

Roast for 20 minutes at 425°F. Reduce the heat to 350°F. and cook another 40 to 45 minutes. Check for doneness by piercing the thigh joint; the juices should run clear. Loosely tent the chicken with aluminum foil and let rest for 10 minutes before carving. Spoon pan drippings over the sliced chicken and serve immediately.

A cream bottle from the Kowloon Dairy, of all places. Somehow, when you think of Hong Kong, where Kowloon is located, cows and dairies aren't the first thing you think of.

BEST-EVER CHICKEN THIGHS

Perfectly delicious and wonderfully easy! If you thought you knew everything there was to know about cooking chicken, think again. This method, originally set forth by Paul Bertolli in his book Cooking by Hand, *was then modified by Melissa Hamilton and Christopher Hirsheimer of Canal House fame. Bertolli called the cooking method "bottom-up cooking." (He should receive a big reward for unleashing it on the world). Essentially you pan fry chicken thighs over low heat for approximately 15 to 20 minutes per side, flipping once only. I further modified it because I wanted a simple pan sauce to serve with the chicken. As far as I'm concerned, this is about as good as food gets. Serves 4.*

1 tablespoon lemon-infused olive oil (page 25) or regular olive oil
4 large chicken thighs
Salt and freshly ground pepper, to taste
⅓ cup dry vermouth or dry white wine
⅓ cup chicken broth
1 teaspoon flour
1 tablespoon butter
Rind from ¼ of a preserved lemon (page 27), lightly rinsed and diced
Lemon wedges and chopped fresh parsley, for garnish

Put olive oil in a heavy skillet (just big enough to accommodate the thighs) over low heat. Salt and pepper the thighs to your taste. Place chicken, skin side down, in the skillet and cook, without fussing with them, for 15 to 20 minutes, or until they reach the desired "brownness." Do not cover pan. Turn thighs over and cook for an additional 15 to 20 minutes. Place chicken on a platter and loosely tent with foil. Increase heat to medium and add flour to the pan juices; whisk to mix and thicken. Add the wine and broth and continue to whisk until it thickens slightly. Whisk in butter and the diced preserved lemon rind at the last minute to preserve their flavor. Place chicken thighs on top of small pools of sauce on serving plates. Garnish with chopped parsley and lemon wedges. Excellent served with risotto or orzo pasta cooked in chicken broth.

The simplicity of this white-on-white scene appeals to me. Hidden under the lemons is the image of an ear of corn — special plates for individual ears of corn on the cob, of course!

'MEYER' LEMON TURKEY PICATTA

I discovered using turkey tenders in this dish by accident – a happy accident as they are better, I think, than the more traditional veal scallops – not to mention a fraction of the cost. Turkey tenderloins are the long, tender strips of white meat hidden under the turkey breast. Serves 4 generously.

2 large 'Meyer' lemons
4 boneless, skinless turkey tenderloins, sliced into ⅜-inch thick slices
Kosher or sea salt, to taste
Freshly ground black pepper, to taste
¼ cup flour in a shaker or sieve
4 tablespoons olive oil
1 small shallot, minced (about 2 tablespoons)
½ cup chicken broth
½ cup dry Vermouth
2 tablespoons capers, drained
3 tablespoons unsalted butter, softened
2 tablespoons fresh parsley, minced

Slice half of one lemon into ⅛-inch slices. Juice the remaining 1½ lemons; you should have about ¼ cup. Set aside.

Season both sides of the turkey tender slices with salt and pepper. Dust tenders with flour on all sides.

Heat 2 tablespoons of olive oil in a large, heavy-bottomed skillet over medium-high heat until hot. Sauté the turkey slices approximately 1 minute per side. Add the minced shallot and cook, stirring, for 1 minute. Add the chicken broth, dry vermouth and lemon slices. Allow to cook until lemon slices are softened.

Add the capers and lemon juice; reduce slightly to concentrate flavors. Remove pan from heat and swirl in the butter until it melts and thickens the sauce. Sprinkle with parsley and serve immediately over a bed of steamed rice, orzo pasta, or couscous.

California neighbors: citrus and oleanders — both very content in our Mediterranean climate.

FINNISH SUNSHINE CAKE

This is a variation of the cake my Finnish grandmother baked for me every time I visited her in San Francisco, except she used fresh orange juice in place of 'Meyer' lemons. I think she'd like it this way. Adapted from The Complete Scandinavian Cookbook *by Alice B. Johnson. Serves 8.*

For the cake:
6 eggs, separated
1 teaspoon cream of tartar
⅛ teaspoon salt
1¼ cup sugar
Grated zest of 1 'Meyer' lemon
2 teaspoons 'Meyer' lemon juice
1 cup cake flour, sifted

For the icing:
1¼ cups powdered sugar, sifted
2 tablespoons whipping cream
2 tablespoons lemon juice
Grated lemon zest for garnish

Preheat oven to 350 degrees F. Lightly grease a 9-inch springform pan. Beat the egg whites in a large bowl for a minute or so until frothy. Add the cream of tartar and salt and continue to beat until stiff. Add the sugar, then beat until stiff again.

In a small bowl, beat the egg yolks. Add the whites, lemon zest, and lemon juice and carefully fold in. Fold in the flour just until incorporated, then pour the batter into the prepared pan. Bake for 40 minutes, or until a toothpick inserted in the middle comes out clean. Set on a wire rack to cool, then run a knife along the perimeter and remove from the pan.

While the cake cools, make the icing. In a medium bowl, whisk the powdered sugar with the cream and lemon juice until smooth. Spread the icing on the cake and garnish with a little more lemon zest.

My favorite cutting board from Thailand. Made of super hard, dense tamarind wood, this round cutting board also has a handy handle, making it easy to take the whole thing over to a pot rather than bringing the pot to the cutting board.

SUSAN'S 'MEYER' LEMON TART

This is my friend, Susan's, formerly secret recipe. She says it's the best and easiest tart dough out there – and very French!

For the crust:
1 cup powdered sugar
1¾ cup flour
Pinch of salt
9 tablespoons unsalted butter, softened
1 large egg

Mix all dry ingredients. Place the softened butter in a food processor and process until smooth. Add dry ingredients and egg to butter. Process quickly until dough forms a mass; do not overmix. Divide dough in half, shape into disks; wrap individually in plastic wrap. Freeze one for later use and let the other rest in refrigerator at least two hours or up to 24 hours.

For the lemon curd:
Grated zest and juice of 3 to 4 'Meyer' lemons
3 eggs
½ cup sugar
3 tablespoons unsalted butter, in small pieces

Put lemon zest and juice in the top of a double boiler and whisk in the eggs. Add the sugar and butter and place pan over just simmering water; water should not touch the bottom of the top pan. Whisk constantly until the butter is melted and the mixture is thick and smooth – about 10 to 15 minutes. Remove the pan and cover with plastic wrap directly on top of lemon curd; let rest at least 15 minutes.

Roll out dough for a 10-inch tart pan and bake in 325°F oven until golden. Pour in filling and bake for an additional 10 minutes, until just set. Let cool before serving.

This is one of the earliest paintings I did of 'Meyer' lemons, way back in 2006. It was done on colored watercolor paper, using gouache rather than watercolors.

50/50 FROZEN
'MEYER' LEMON TREATS

Serving lemon granita in a hollowed-out lemon has a distinctively retro feel to it, but it never fails to eliclit appreciative words from folks around the table. Why not dial the Way Back Machine way back with a present day take on those 50/50 ice cream bars of your youth? Serves 4.

¼ cup superfine granulated sugar
1¼ cups water
¾ cup 'Meyer' lemon juice (approximately 3 lemons)
Zest from ½ 'Meyer' lemon
Store-bought premium vanilla ice cream
4 whole 'Meyer' lemons
Four mint sprigs for garnish

Cut off the top ⅓ of the lemon (not the stem end) and reserve for the "cap." Carefully hollow out lemons using a grapefruit knife or grapefruit spoon with a serrated edge. You can press the flesh you take out of lemons to make the juice you need. Take a shallow slice off the other end of the lemon so it will sit upright on a plate without tipping over. Be careful not to cut through to the inside of the lemon. Freeze the shells and caps at least one hour or overnight.

Place the water and sugar in a bowl and stir to dissolve. Add the lemon juice and zest. Stir. Pour into a shallow pan and freeze for approximately 2 hours. When ready to serve, remove from freezer and scrape the granita crystals from the pan to create a kind of slush. Place the frozen lemon shells on individual plates. Fill with alternating layers of vanilla ice cream and lemon granita. Top with the reserved lemon caps and a sprig of mint. Serve immediately.

I'm always on the lookout for interesting plates and platters that might complement 'Meyer' lemons. This one, with its unusual black-and-white decoration, really fit the bill.

'MEYER' LEMON AND MACADAMIA MACAROONS

The flavor of these macaroons is way out of proportion to the ease of making them. The recipe started out as one from Gourmet magazine, morphed a little over time, but has remained a perennial favorite for anybody who's tried it. The original instructions included the line "the cookies can be stored in an airtight container at room temperature for up to a week." Right. They'll be gone in about five minutes.

3 large egg whites, at room temperature
½ cup granulated sugar
1 tablespoon 'Meyer' lemon zest
¼ teaspoon salt
One 14-ounce package sweetened flaked coconut
36 whole salted macadamia nuts

Preheat oven to 350ºF. Position rack in the middle position. Line two heavy cookie sheets with parchment paper, silicone baking mats, or use non-stick cookie sheets.

Whisk together the egg whites, sugar, lemon zest, and salt until frothy. Using a fork, mix in the coconut thoroughly.

Using a tablespoon measure, drop the cookie dough on the baking sheets. The cookies can be placed fairly close together as they don't spread much. Using damp fingers, smooth the dough. Press one macadamia nut onto the top of each cookie.

Bake one sheet at a time, turning the cookie sheet once halfway through the baking time – about 8 minutes. Cookies are done when the bottom edges turn a deep, golden brown. Start checking for doneness after 12 minutes or so. Ovens vary, but cookies should be done in a total cooking time of 15 to 20 minutes. Allow cookies to cool on the baking sheets set on wire racks.

Footed bowls, like the one above, are used to hold offerings in Buddhist temples in Thailand. Would Buddha approve of the 'Meyer' lemons as an offering? I think so.

'MEYER' LEMON AMOR POLENTA

The origins of this recipe, at least in this household, have been lost in the mists of time. It became a favorite after the first time I tried it, decades ago. I love it just as it is, especially with a good cup of coffee, or excellent topped with any fresh berry.

⅔ cup butter, softened
2 cups powdered sugar
1 tablespoon 'Meyer' lemon zest
1 teaspoon vanilla
2 eggs plus 1 egg yolk
1¼ cups flour
⅓ cup cornmeal
Powdered sugar for dusting, if desired

Preheat oven to 325ºF.

Cream the butter and powdered sugar in a large bowl. Add the lemon zest, vanilla, eggs and extra egg yolk to the creamed butter and sugar mixture and mix thoroughly.

Add the flour and cornmeal to the butter-sugar-egg mixture and mix well. Pour batter into a buttered saddle pan* dusted with cornmeal. Bake for one hour and 15 minutes.

* *"And what exactly is a 'saddle pan'?"* you might ask. Right after I wrote the words "saddle pan" I realized that I didn't really know what one was, only that I had one and it only gets used when I make amor polenta. Thanks to the power of the web, I found out that a saddle pan is also known as a *"Rehrücken"* pan. And that *"rehrücken"* means "saddle of venison cake" in German. Before we enter the arena of too-much-information, just think of a tin can cut in half lengthwise and you get the general idea of its shape. If you don't have one, a loaf pan works fine.

I'll tell you one thing – after doing the paintings for this book, I definitely had a new-found appeciation for the craftspeople who apply the designs and patterns on porcelain.

'MEYER' LEMON BUTTERMILK PUDDING CAKE WITH FRESH BERRIES

I'm a sucker for pudding cakes and this one is particularly good. It originally appeared on the Epicurious website many years ago. Over time, it's undergone a few tweaks which, I think, have made a very good thing even better.

1½ cups buttermilk
1 cup granulated sugar, divided
4 large egg yolks
⅓ cup 'Meyer' lemon juice
1 tablespoon 'Meyer' lemon zest
¼ cup all-purpose flour
¼ cup unsalted butter, melted
⅛ teaspoon salt
4 large egg whites

Assorted fresh berries

Preheat the oven to 350°F.

Butter 8- by 8-inch glass baking dish. Blend buttermilk, ½ cup sugar, egg yolks, lemon juice and zest, flour, butter, and salt in a blender until smooth. Transfer the buttermilk mixture to a medium bowl. Using an electric mixer, beat egg whites in a large bowl until soft peaks form. Gradually add remaining sugar and beat until stiff but not dry. Gently fold buttermilk mixture, one-third at a time, into the beaten egg whites. Batter will be runny.

Pour batter into prepared dish. Place dish in a larger roasting pan. Pour enough hot water into the roasting pan to come halfway up the sides of the baking dish. Bake until entire top is evenly browned and cake moves very slightly in the center but feels springy to the touch, about 45 minutes.

Cool cake completely in baking dish on rack. Refrigerate until cold, at least 3 hours and up to 6 hours. Spoon pudding cake out into shallow bowls and top with fresh berries.

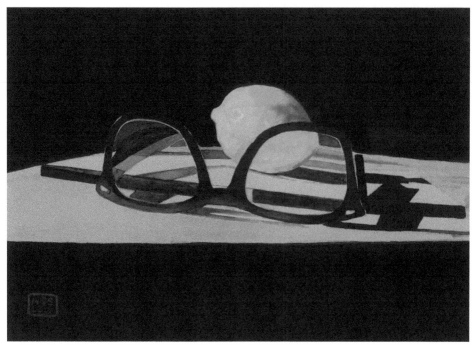

Finally found the painting I was looking for: The Last One!

'MEYER' LEMON SHAKER PIE

From its humble beginnings, the Shaker lemon pie has passed into something approaching cult status. Three things about this recipe: 1) It's wonderful, 2) it's not mine – it belongs to the rather remarkable Deb Perelman of the equally remarkable website www.smittenkitchen.com and 3) kids will probably hate it and adults will probably love it. Let's just say it's intense.

2 large 'Meyer' lemons, zested first and then very thinly sliced
2 cups granulated sugar
¼ teaspoon salt
4 eggs, lightly beaten
4 tablespons butter, melted
3 tablespoons all-purpose flour
1 egg white
Coarse sugar, for sprinkling
Dough for one double-crust pie

Thoroughly wash and dry lemons. Finely grate lemon zest into a bowl. Using a mandoline, slice lemons as paper thin as you can possibly get them; remove and discard seeds. Add slices to zest and toss with sugar and salt. Cover and set aside at room temperature for 24 hours.

Preheat the oven to 425°F. Roll out half the dough ⅛-inch thick on a lightly-floured surface, fit it into a 9-inch pie plate, and trim the edge, leaving a ½-inch overhang.

Mix the macerated lemon-sugar mixture with the four eggs, melted butter and flour until combined well. Pour into prepared pie shell.

Roll out the remaining dough into a 12-inch round on a lightly-floured surface, drape it over the filling, and trim it, leaving a 1-inch overhang. Fold the overhang under the bottom crust, pressing the edge to seal it, and crimp the edge. Beat one egg white until frothy and brush over pie crust, then sprinkle with coarse sugar. Cut slits in the crust with a sharp knife, forming steam vents, and bake the pie in the middle of the oven for 25 minutes. Reduce the temperature to 350°F. and bake the pie for 20 to 25 minutes more, or until the crust is golden. Let the pie cool on a rack and serve it warm.

continued from page 51

Slice the cornbread in half horizontally – yes, it *can* be done, using a long, serrated bread knife. Cut the sliced cornbread into two rectangles large enough to accomodate the scallops. Gently butter the slices of cornbread and toast in a toaster oven (it is too crumbly and delicate to toast in a toaster). Reserve toasts.

Whisk the cream until it forms soft peaks. Reserve. Place yolks, lemon juice, zest, and salt in a medium heatproof bowl set over a pan of simmering water (not boiling – if the water is too hot the egg yolks will simply form curds) or a double boiler. Do not let bottom of bowl touch the water. Whisk constantly, until the mixture has thickened to the consistancy of mayonnaise, about 4 minutes. Remove the bowl from the heat, and gently fold in the whipped cream. Reserve.

Add the scallops to the pan and cook over medium-high heat for 1 to 2 minutes per side. Do not overcook. Set aside.

To serve, place the cornbread toasts on plate. Add the scallops on top and cover with the shallot, pepper, corn mixture. Smother the combination with the sauce sabayon and serve immediately. Prepare to be delighted.

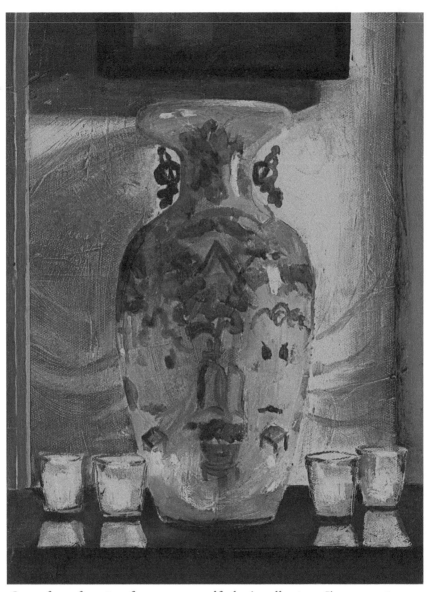

One of my favorites from my grandfather's collection. I'm not quite sure how, but this one – thankfully – survived the big earthquake of August 2014 here in Napa.

A Note on the Illustrations

As a resource for the paintings in this book, I had the good fortune of inheriting two generations' worth of blue-and-white Chinese and Japanese porcelain. Both my grandfather, Captain Nels A. Sinnes and my father, Captain Alfred E. Sinnes, spent decades in the Far East during their service in the Merchant Marines. Virtually all of the pieces were presented to them as gifts when they arrived at one port or another, some of them dating back to the 1920s. It seemed a natural combination – that a citrus found in Asia should be painted on Asian porcelain. What a pleasure to make this project a multi-generational voyage with a couple of great mates I had the pleasure of calling "Grandpa" and "Dad."

•   •   •

In working on this book, I debated whether to include only paintings painted specifically for this book, or to include paintings done

My grandgather, Capt. Nels Sinnes, aboard the S.S. Samoa, December 1941, shortly before being torpedoed by a Japanese submarine off the coast of Cape Mendocino, California – but that's another story …

My father, Capt. Alfred Sinnes, arriving Singapore from Manila, S.S. Idaho, Voyage 47W. States Steamship Company. December 18, 1977.

prior to when the idea for this book had even occurred to me. In the end, I decided to include the earlier paintings as I thought a progression would be more interesting – especially considering that I started using oil paints and moved to watercolors as time went on.

I have been both influenced and inspired by the English artist (living in France), Julian Merrow-Smith. He was one of the originators of the "painting-a-day" movement and remains one of its best practitioners. His beautiful work can be seen at www.shiftinglight.com.

As I mentioned in one of the captions, I do virtually all of my painting at the kitchen table in my old house in the Old Town section of Napa. I've tried other locations, but I always gravitate back to the kitchen. It's not very convenient – especially when I want to play cards, eat a meal, or any of the other things one normally does at a kitchen table. But it's homey and warm, the light is good, and with NPR on the radio, quite companionable.

Acknowledgements

Many thanks to Patty and her amazingly productive 'Meyer' lemon bush (which is about the size of a Volkswagen) and all the lemons it provided for many of the recipes in this book – not to mention the lemon marmalade she/it produced like magic at the last minute. Throughout the process of writing this book, Amy has been not only a culinary inspiration but a contributor of recipes – thank you Amy. Thanks also to Saul and Karen for pitching in in both the kitchen and at the dining room table; it's good to have fun while you work! And it's good to have friends like Lance who know as much about 'Meyer' lemons as anyone and who emails you right back when you have even the most esoteric of questions. Last but hardly least, thank you Michèle for your peerless editorial skills and for keeping me from stumbling over myself in the English Department. Thanks to all of you for your cheerful assistance.

Prints
are Available

All 36 of the paintings I did as illustrations for this book are available as prints. Each print is individually produced on a large format inkjet printer, reproduced from digital photographs of the original artwork. The inks used are archival, printed on heavy watercolor paper. All prints are 4½ by 6½ inches, matted in a white 8-inch by 10-inch mat, which is a standard frame size. The prints are signed and dated. If you'd like to have the print inscribed, just let me know.

Prints are $40 each, plus $6 postage and handling, mailed via Priority Mail. If you are interested, please send me an email at acorts@me.com.

Thanks!

A. Cont Sumer

CPSIA information can be obtained
at www.ICGtesting.com
Printed in the USA
BVHW091010161121
621766BV00018B/769